SHAPES

Optimize Your Portfolio by Implementing a
Technology Evaluation Model

ERIK BOE

ISBN-13: 978-1499124859
ISBN-10: 1499124856

Dedication

I dedicate this book to my colleagues who worked with me in the Core Technology Group at Adobe. Their openness and support made it possible to explore, experiment, and finally arrive at a solution for technology investment decisions. The core of the group is no longer, but the people and the spirit of the group are still at Adobe.

Contents

Preface   i

Acknowledgments   ii

1   Why Do You Need a Model?   1

2   What Is a Model?   6

3   How Do You Create a Model?   10

4   The Parts of the Model   13

5   How Does the Model Work?   20

6   How Do You Implement the Model?   32

7   Going Beyond the Evaluation Model   42

About the Author   46

Preface

I started my career at Apple in the international software group. One of our goals was to make a release of the Macintosh operating system support multiple languages. At the time it was common practice to ship the English version first and other versions later, sometimes more than a year later. In order to achieve this goal, it quickly became clear that we needed to present convincing information consistently throughout the company. We needed to create a model for making decisions about what languages to support, while accounting for investment and returns. Ever since, I have approached complicated decisions in large groups by creating models, which make it possible to speak a common language.

The technology evaluation model was formed by years of experimentation. It is my hope that this book will make you, the reader, successful in portfolio management. The concepts in this book are easy to understand and adapt. The challenge is to balance the implementation against the everyday demands of a fast-moving development organization. My hope is that you can use this book as a guide for creating your own model and moving forward with implementation. It is not the model itself that is critical to success, but rather the amount of dialogue that follows.

Acknowledgments

The concept behind this book was developed while I was working at Apple and later Adobe. The management team of the Core Technology Group at Adobe used this approach to make and communicate technology investment decisions that affected the whole company.

I would like to thank Frits Habermann, Ben Bauermeister, Paul Holland, and Ranjit Desai. Over the years, we spent countless hours together struggling with technology investment decisions. After an especially long session in Seattle, we achieved evaluation enlightenment. All the pieces fell into place, and we gained collective clarity on how to decide which technologies would fit into our portfolio. It became a powerful tool we used for years to come.

1

Why Do You Need a Model?

New ideas are all around us. They spring to life in the midst of busy days. The collective ingenuity of motivated groups can make anything happen. However, separate agendas, lack of dialogue and competing goals fight against harnessing greatness. A technology evaluation model is about *mindshare*. It allows a group to focus. It is not about predicting the future, but rather capturing energy. Focus combined with energy drive innovation. A technology evaluation model is a simple way of fueling the innovation pipeline, the engine that builds products customers will love.

Every day I wonder if I am working on something that will make a difference. Will my technology one day make its way into a great product or service? Will it improve our society? Will it in some small way make a positive impact? Is there something I can do that will help me make the best possible investment decision as early in the development cycle as possible? What should I be looking for? Is there a way of increasing my batting average?

This is a challenge in almost every industry. What makes people like a particular movie? What is it about a song that makes it the next big hit? What will the next miracle drug do? In order to optimize our chances of success, we break the question into smaller parts. We look at each part individually and compare it to something we know has been successful in the past. For example, if you want to make a great movie you look for successful actors, talented scriptwriters, an intriguing place to film the movie, the best makeup artists, and so on. Every part looks great. Will the sum be great? We simply won't know until the movie has been released. And even then, it also matters what other movies you are competing against at that time.

"Which investment will give the greatest results?" is one of the most difficult questions to answer. Some people know all the answers. Some are looking for answers. Sometimes, it is best not to answer, as we have no way of making a decision. Occasionally we stumble upon a path that works. Agile and Lean development methodologies may help us get quicker and more regular feedback, but they are not predictive of success. They are designed to narrow that gap in time from investment to results. Vision, mission, and goals are meant to guide us through difficult choices by painting a space to operate within. Strategy and road maps tell us what to implement and how to do it.

What is the tool of choice in regard to investment decisions? There are probably as many of them as there are companies. Of those I have seen, most are not formal, documented, enforced, or widely understood. It is very much like making sausage. The outcome might be phenomenal, but the process is best hidden. If you happen to know of a great way to predict success, why would you share it? Why would you show your competitors your advantage? It is the competitive nature of achieving product success that makes it challenging to establish portfolio management as a discipline.

Portfolio Management
I will put forth that a holistic portfolio management discipline can complement most development practices in a high-tech company. It does not need to compete with activities that are working well. It should help to organize a complex situation and make investment decisions as natural as apple pie. It should not be a spreadsheet exercise done by one person over a weekend. It is not about numbers or formulas. Rather, it is something that must be integrated into the everyday life of product development teams. Therefore, it must be easy, transparent, and shared widely. And even more important, everyone must be accountable for adhering to decisions made within the framework.

If you already have a tool and are happy with it, then use it as a starting point. If not, look around in the company to see if you can find something in your development, project, or financial groups that will fit your needs. In this book, I outline a simple model that can be incorporated into other tools or set up using lightweight solutions such as wikis, web pages, or online documents.

What is an investment decision? For the most part it is a decision about how to allocate time or money. Money to pay for new technologies, people's time to work on projects. How are investment decisions normally made in a company? It varies. In some, one person makes all the decisions and informs the teams. In others, teams are empowered to invent and put forth new solutions. Sometimes, investment decisions are shared; other times, you stumble upon them. I put forth that most organizations appreciate knowing how projects are funded. It helps teams understand the direction the company is heading. While most teams want to be part of the latest and greatest, you will always have some teams doing maintenance work. This is natural. There is no way of hiding it. If you invest somewhere, you must reduce elsewhere unless you have unlimited funds or you are in a period of growth. Expansionary times do not last forever; they always end.

What is a portfolio? It is a collection of stuff. In high-tech this often means a set of products or services. A product or service is something you place in front of users. They come with benefits that—you hope—will make them willing to pay. In this book, I focus on the word *technologies*. I use this word when referring to the portfolio. Why? In my case, my group developed technologies that were incorporated into products and services. Technology for us was an effective unit to manage. Your unit of measure can be anything. It can be products, services, sections of products, or technologies, or you can have all of these.

For me, a technology is the underpinning of like features. A project is a time-bound set of activities that eventually results in new or better features that, you hope, end up in a product or service that users will buy. The reason we manage a portfolio is that we want it to change it, to move it toward results we like, namely, happy customers. So in the end, our technology investment decisions are what fuels a company's revenue growth.

A portfolio must be anchored in something. It must be framed by a problem, a customer set, technologies, skills, or new ideas. If not, you could end up with everything, which might be fine if you are exploring and have unlimited funds and time. Most of us do not. A framing can change over time. It is not meant to be everlasting. If business conditions change, insight is gained, or a new opportunity opens up, the portfolio should adapt. It should, however, remain anchored in this new direction. If you at any time lose your anchor, you lose time and money. And you may also see that your group loses its motivation because of too many distractions. Here are a few simple framings:

- "We want to make it easy for our customers to file their taxes."
- "We want to make video-transcoding usable for anyone."
- "We are graphics technology experts."

But even these are broad. The best approach here is to consider how much time and money you want to invest into exploring versus targeting. In other words, invest in many as opposed to a narrower set of technologies. Once you have your framing, communicate it to your organization's people. They will love you for it.

Just because you have framed your portfolio does not mean you are not looking for new ideas. It means that you are focused. It means you want your organization to focus as well. It means that most of your time and effort should be on achieving goals as outlined by your portfolio. You should be open to new ideas. But you can't let them disrupt your organization until you have considered them as a viable path. At that point, invest accordingly.

Who owns the portfolio data? Everyone does. If you want to manage your portfolio, meaning improve and move it forward, then everyone must participate. Access to technology portfolio data is a constant need in a fast-moving company. There are daily requests for information. What is our road map? How many people do we have available who can help out with the latest customer-reported issue? Will this affect our next deliverable? What is the risk of moving groups around? Any one of these questions is easier to answer if you are working in a small team. When you belong to a larger organization, they all become more difficult. Therefore, in larger groups, you must set aside time and effort to capture, maintain, and share the portfolio data. It is the foundation for many of the preceding questions. At the end of the day, it is always about priorities—what is important and when. And those answers you find in your portfolio.

How do you capture and show your portfolio? There are many different ways of sharing. It all depends on who the audience is and what they want to know. The important part of a portfolio is that you have all the data available and can create different views at any time for any request. That means one person cannot keep the data in his or her computer; the data must be available to all in a central location.

If you have other data you are using related to your portfolio analysis, you must designate the sources. It can quickly become a nightmare if several sources claim ownership of the same data. A typical problem is information related to the number of employees and open positions. You often end up using this data when you are looking at your overall portfolio investment and profile. Employee data is found in many places within a company. Groups use it for different purposes. You must be clear on where your source is. If not, you will eventually be faced with data from a different source that compete with your information and could destroy any message you want to relay. If you already have a solution for tracking and reporting on projects and products, you could augment it with portfolio attributes. Much of the data you generate from your portfolio can be used in several contexts. Ideas for how to distribute portfolio information are discussed later in the book.

A portfolio solution has several parts. At its core is a model that helps the organization evaluate technologies. It has a method for capture and display of content and a set of rules and expected behaviors. This book focuses on creating the core model and sharing portfolio information, and it discusses ideas around how to implement a portfolio solution. The model discussed in this book worked well for my particular situation. I fully expect that different companies will have specific circumstances that need to become part of an evaluation model. Therefore, use this book as guide for how to establish and use a model and plan to adapt it for your specific needs.

A technology evaluation model directs energy toward areas best set up for success.

2

What Is a Model?

A model is, in a sense, an escape from reality. It is a way of emulating the world by simplification. You ignore content you don't want to think about. Why do this? Because the world is complicated. There are just too many variables and attributes to map out in order to create a near-perfect model. Micro- and macroeconomics are all about models. Our financial systems are built on complicated models trying to optimize return on investment. Gambling in any form, including life and health insurance, is all about the probability of an occurrence taking place. A recent trend online is tracking Internet users in order to better understand them and optimize the possibility of presenting them with an offer they can't refuse. Another trend is to get to know them better than they know themselves so products and services can reach them "almost before" a buying decision has been made.

If we have the ability to create sophisticated models, why can't we build one that will tell us what products and features will appeal to users? Human behavior is complex. We are still trying to understand our brains and how they work. On one hand, we are very close to our animal ancestry in our desire to survive and conquer. On the other hand, we have an amazing ability to comprehend the universe we are part of. Packaging human behavior into a computer science college degree to prepare our future software developers and designers is a big task. Nonetheless, the software engineers and designers are creating solutions to meet our needs. They have to work closely with marketing and sales to make their products profitable. In order to get all this done, companies are created. A company that wants to grow will be under constant financial pressure. We live in a competitive, global society that is expanding in capabilities and possibilities. It is a little overwhelming to try to capture all this in a model that can predict product success and failure.

The software industry is moving toward rapidly building features that are released to users as soon as they are completed. If the feature works, then great! Build more like that. If it does not work well, then drop it. With more and more solutions moving online, a frequent delivery model has been cast upon us. Sometimes, this is great; sometimes, it is terrible, as it forces us to constantly learn a different way of getting the same task accomplished! Regardless, we are all part of a trial-and-error software-delivery model.

So instead of focusing on a narrow set of features, it is easier to model technology areas that are best set up for success. A technology evaluation model should look for factors that are typically present for a successful technology. However, you have to select as few as possible to make the model easy to use. A simple model allows people to have focused discussions. It allows them to talk about variables and scores in a rather efficient manner. Once a model is understood, participants can frame their discussions based upon the model in order to analyze and gain deeper understanding of the real world. However, a model needs to make sense. It must be closely aligned with what people understand and accept. If it competes with common sense, the model will not gain traction. It is fine, however, if what you learn from the model is surprising. As long as the model is accepted, the outcome must also be considered a possibility. If not, then it may be time to change the model or accept its limitations.

By the way, changing the model as you learn more is normal. When we created our model, it did not start out as you see it in this book. We only had a few variables. They were leverage and bullets-on-the-box (new features). These would then guide our investment decisions. Over time, we ran into many challenging situations and added to the model to avoid future problems. One tough item to add to our model was *overhead*, which was the amount of time and effort we had to expect to invest when coordinating and communicating to a large number of stakeholders. As engineers, we often focus on developing features, and we pride ourselves on overcoming complexity. Overhead has real costs and can be a leading factor in product failure, so it became part of our model.

Allow your model to grow as you learn. When you see a failing technology that was ranked high, ask why. The more frequently you review your portfolio, the faster you learn.

A portfolio evaluation model is not about math. It is not science nor is it art. It is about documenting the collective knowledge of a group. It can be qualitative or it can be quantitative. It can be objective or it can be subjective. It is a memory bank that is organized into categories defined by you. It is a temporary view of the world around you and a tool to help you quickly review a large amount of data in order to make decisions that will help your group become successful. But do not make the model king. The numbers are not meant to hold contributors hostage. A model captures the current thinking. It is not meant to paint a picture of the future. That is where analysis and planning come in.

The numbers themselves are relative. It is about comparing them to other technologies. You assign a score by saying it is the same, better, or worse than something else. The results are meant to provide insights that can be discussed further. The results might initially be wrong, but if they are, they should set you on a course to collect more data. The results may be too good, forcing you to think twice about the assumptions you have made. Perhaps it is sunny-day planning that requires additional input.

Some people are uncomfortable placing values on variables in a model. For one, it does not feel natural or fair. It may force someone to make a decision he or she is not quite sure about. This can best be overcome by walking the group through the whole model. If, at the end, you look back and your decisions and numbers do not seem to make sense, then something went wrong. If not, then you have shown that the numbers are just a way to help you to get to the end.

Using a model may shine the light on motivations that were not well understood before. Pet projects often fall into this category. It is normal to have those. There are times when the world has changed based upon the strong belief and determination of a few. If you want to have special projects, use different criteria. Just make that clear to everyone who is looking at your portfolio. The worst thing to do in this case is to dress up those technologies to make them look better.

Sharing

You don't have to send your models out to the world. They are meant to be tools to help you make decisions. They are mental notes, not the final results. How do you share the final results? We decided to make it very simple using the highway concept. A technology is on the highway, entering, or exiting. The categories we initially defined were:

- On-Ramp
- Highway: High, Medium, Low
- Off-Ramp

Because most technologies ended up on the highway, we needed to create a few more subcategories. We used high, medium, and low to indicate investment levels. However, we quickly ran into problems with this because nobody wanted to be in the low or even the medium category. The competitive nature of people showed up. So we defined a more neutral way of communicating that looked like this:

- On-Ramp
- Highway: Invest, Steady-State, Maintain
- Off-Ramp

Invest was a category of technologies that were new and growing in use and investment. In steady-state, we allowed any type of work to be done as limited by the current team size. In maintain, we restricted efforts to critical fixes. It was about keeping the technology as-is.

The highway concept made it simple to communicate across groups. We did not have to dive into the evaluation model very often. We could focus on the results of the model. But we still had to make sure that our portfolio was aligned with the business goals of the company.

A model is a simplification of the world to allow focus and improve decision making.

3

How Do You Create a Model?

Creating a model is not accomplished from the top down. It starts with trying to make sense of a product development world overflowing with data, much of which is not organized nor connected. Most of it is only available to a few. One of the biggest problems you encounter in a larger organization is that most of the available data is outdated. Much of what you easily find has been captured for a particular purpose and placed on a wiki; it was not meant to be part of an overall company data set. Then you have enterprise solutions run by IT organizations. Very often data here is overstructured and not used by the development community. Regardless, look at what is available and what is important for your organization. If it can easily be harvested or organized, then consider using it. Start collecting, but make it simple. Use small sample sets to experiment with before making any big commitments. Asking everyone in the company to log his or her time against a task may not be what you need. Over time it will become clear what is useful and what is not.

Sometimes, we get attached to available data and use it to make all kinds of decisions. It is surprising how often important decisions are built upon the most fleeting of data. Have you ever been asked to provide a detailed road map over the weekend? Or a list of everything all team members are doing? Or which features could be dropped to meet a ship date three weeks out? If you have systems in place with updated content, these are relatively easy tasks. If not, you scramble to put all available data into a presentation with few or weak links to the actual state of affairs in the development groups. The less time you have to collect a new data set, the less the usability of the data is. Reliable data is generated as part of an everyday process. This ensures that everyone knows how to gather, use, and present the data. It is almost impossible to make good investment decisions without a system that is updated and supported by the whole organization.

There is no right or wrong way of building a model. Therefore, make it your way! In other words, build your model based on what is important for you. If you believe that every product should make a customer happy, then make that part of your model. If you think that innovation comes from hard work trying to solve tough problems, then incorporate that into your model. At the same time, include elements you do not believe in. For example, if there are too many people trying to solve too many problems in too little time, stay away from those projects. In other words, build into your model that some types of projects are prone to failure. Include that certain types of projects require a higher level of time and resource commitments. Don't forget to include what you have seen to be successful in the past. Perhaps you have seen a small focused group of highly motivated individuals come up with a new solution in a very short time. If so, think about what you can extract from that. Is it team size? Is it their understanding of the problem? Is it their skill level? Is it mostly because they are motivated? Did they have a strong leader? You decide. In the end, it should be something that everyone in the group is willing to accept as a variable in the model.

A model based upon untested variables has little value. It is only after variables are validated that they becomes useful. Thus, do not spend too much time perfecting the model unless you have populated it with data and can actually see that it makes a difference. My experience is that data will help you create a model that makes sense. The data will tell you what you should spend time focusing on. I remember once when we created a set of variables to help measure a group's success. The group members picked variables and values that they knew they could achieve with little effort. In other words, there was no point in measuring it. Nothing would change; you could not make any decisions based upon the data because it remained constant.

We created our model to meet several goals. First, we wanted to be aligned with the overall direction of the company. Whatever the company was trying to achieve, we needed to support. In our case, that meant we needed to support important goals of flagship products. If at any time we ran into funding shortfalls, the first to go would be efforts not seen as critical to the company. Second, we needed to support the core value of the group, which was deep technical expertise. We were thought leaders in complicated technologies. We could make anything come alive. It might take time and effort, but we could make it happen. Third, we needed to make it cost effective. As with most groups, managing cost was critical to our long-term survival. And lastly, we wanted to avoid getting stuck with old technologies in maintenance mode. We wanted to be working on technologies that were new, exciting, and growing. You could argue that more attributes were needed. Yes, you could create a longer list, but you would end up with an overflow of data. If you cannot collect it efficiently, it will be costly to maintain. But more important, it will be difficult to have conversations in your own group or with your customers if you are talking about too many variables.

A model is created through dialogue in order to capture the group's collective knowledge.

4

The Parts of the Model

There are probably infinite ways of creating a model to help you make decisions. In this book, I will describe how we defined our model. It will not fit everyone. The best model for you is dependent upon your specific situation. You should take this model and adjust it to your group or company. There will likely be common parts and parts that are very different. But understanding this model will allow you to have a framework for creating one that will work for you.

We had many variables that we grouped into four areas. The four areas we arrived at were:

- Cost Efficiency
- Skill Set
- Partnership
- Life Cycle

In order to make the model work, we had to arrange a high score as being good, meaning it was what we were seeking. A low score was bad, something we were trying to avoid. In the model, that may mean that the actual number associated with one variable could be high while the score was low. At the same time, another variable could have a low number while the score was high. Keep in mind that this is not a math formula. It is a system for assigning values to items you are considering when you are about to make a decision. How you arrive at these scores is up to you. The systems will work as long as you are consistent. In our case, that meant that the same people were present for most of the scoring sessions.

Cost Efficiency

Let's take a look at each of the four areas. First, we have cost efficiency. This is about cost and effort. Is it even possible to play in this space? Is the barrier for entry too high? And what is the potential for return? Hence, the phrase *cost efficiency*. In this category, we had three variables:

SCORE	0	5	10
Team Size	≥ 15	8–10	2–3
Overhead	High	Medium	Low
Value	None	Medium	High

The team size is about how many people were needed to make this solution a reality. The smaller the team, the better. However, a team size that was too small might jeopardize the project. Say it only required one person to get this done. If this was a solution that was meant to last or could have a big impact, then what would happen if that person left the company? So in most cases, we would not consider something that only required one person. Of course, you could work around this by sharing the work among several people. In general, two to three people were a small investment, while more than fifteen was considered large. Here, you should adjust the numbers to fit your organization. Perhaps two hundred is a small number for you. We used team size as a key indicator of cost, as it often accounts for 80 percent or more of total development cost.

Overhead was the amount of effort it would take in coordination and communication. Many groups being affected required more effort. Also, if there was controversy or opposition, that would make the overhead larger. We would assess overhead as a relative measure from small to large.

Value is in the eye of the beholder; hence, we referred to this as *perceived value*. It was sometimes impossible to measure value, but if the leadership had articulated that solutions in a certain space were important, that would result in a higher perceived value as compared to other areas. We would often refer to it as a strategic investment. If you have the ability to assign specific values, such as projected sales or growth, then use that. Another way of thinking about this category is return on investment, or ROI.

Skill Set

The second area was skill set. This is about what we knew and what we could do. If we had the ability to drive our own solutions, then that for us was an important indicator of future success. If it required entry into an unknown technology, that carried more risk. If we had a choice, we would stay close to what we already knew, or that for which we had a defined path of learning or obtaining the required skill set. The more we had to learn, the longer it would take before we could even start making an impact.

SCORE	0	5	10
High Science	None	Medium	High
Ownership	None	Shared	Full
Expertise	Low	Medium	High

High science was cool stuff that we liked to do because it was challenging. For us, that meant we had to apply hard-learned skills and effort to get something done. It was not about creating a new web-based feature over the weekend. It was about solving tough problems. Sometimes, this could take a long time (months or years); other times, it took only weeks. Ownership was about the ability to influence the solution. If someone else owned or competed against us, that was considered less desirable. Expertise was about what we were capable of doing or our ability to gain the necessary expertise. If a problem required a totally new set of skills that we could not acquire anytime soon, then we rated it low.

Partnership

The third area was partnership. There are different ways of thinking about this. We looked at it from both reaching a larger number of partners and the dependencies on others delivering solutions to us.

SCORE	0	3.3	5	6.6	10
Platforms	None	1		2	≥ 3
Leverage	None	5	10	15	≥ 20
Dependencies	≥ 3	2		1	None

At the time, we used platform as a variable because it was important to the company. We had three platforms: Flash, PDF, and Creative Suite. All these were instrumental in moving the company forward over the years. Another way of looking it could have been desktop, mobile, and hosted services. We used this later as the company moved to a different business model. Leverage was about the number of internal product teams we supported. It is not the only measure of success for a core technology group, but it is one of the key ones. The more use a technology had, the less cost it was for the product teams, the more uniform it became for the users, and the more robust the technology would become. It was robust because a broader user base would report more bugs, ask for more features, and overall demand a high level of service. Our leverage would vary from none (technology not in production yet) to as many as thirty-eight internal product teams using a particular technology. Most technologies were in the ten to fifteen range. You can also use the same approach with external customers. You could simply count them or group them into buckets based upon sales or revenue figures. Lastly, we had dependencies. We had a number of technologies that would require code from other teams, such as PDF coming from Acrobat and the Photoshop library coming from Photoshop. The higher the number of external dependencies, the more challenging it would be for us to control the features, bugs, and schedules.

Life Cycle

The last category was the life cycle of the technology. It was important to understand if this was growing or declining space. Was it already conquered, or were there many opportunities?

SCORE	0	5	10
Maturity	≥ 10 years	Established	New
Growth Potential	None	Medium	Significant
Ecosystem	Defined	Somewhat	Not Defined

The level of maturity for a technology was an indication of future potential. Every technology has a life-span ranging from new, growing, and maturing, to declining and eventually vanishing. For us, a ten-or-more-year-old technology was an indication of a mature one. This number will vary depending on your area. You may consider a three-year-old technology mature. On the flip side, it has been said that a submarine may have a life-span of fifty years; hence, the supply chain has to commit to providing parts and service for this length of time. (I have not validated this number.) In any case, a younger technology has more life ahead of it than behind it. This translates into length of time in which a technology can provide revenue or help other technologies provide revenue. Another way of looking at this is that you don't want to invest time and money to obtain the required skill sets and then find that the technology is declining. With many technologies, even if they are mature, they may pivot. They may be able to be used in a new way or combined into a new solution, or perhaps the people behind the technology have skills that are very relevant for a new generation of this technology.

Therefore, regardless of where you are in the life cycle, it is important to understand whether there is growth ahead or if the technology will stay in maintenance mode for a long period of time. The more growth potential, the better. How you get this information will vary. You may be able to get industry data from research companies, or perhaps you have internal groups that collect this information. If not, you have to rely upon the collective knowledge of the people in your group.

Lastly, we looked at the overall ecosystem in which this technology would be used. If there were many players, that was considered a challenge. If there was one player who controlled the definition and delivery of a competing solution, that was also a challenge. We were drawn to areas with attributes of chaos: no clear winner, no clear solution, and no clear revenue path, but full of opportunities for the right player with the right solutions. That was a space we wanted to play in.

Creating a Picture of the Model
The next graph shows the variables placed into each of the four categories. It is a useful graph for thinking about the bigger picture or introducing the model to a group. You may take this and modify it to fit your needs. You might not end up with twelve variables. It just so happens that we arrived at twelve because of the many things we had to consider given that we were a core technology group in large software company.

The model is visually easy to understand. You are striving to the get the shapes (scores) as close to the edge as possible. You want your portfolio profile to be set up for success as defined by what is important to you with your selected variables.

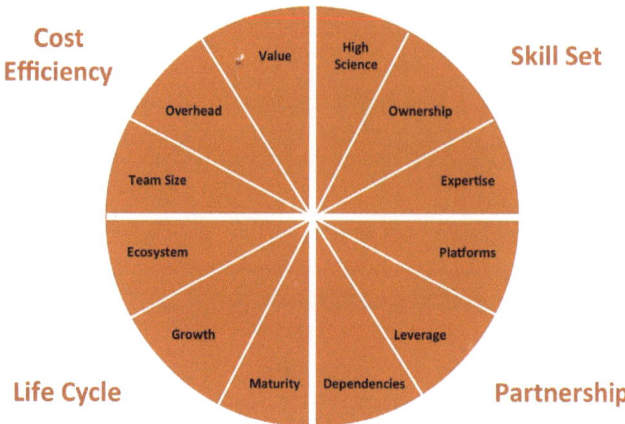

For each area, we would look at the overall score. If it was high, that was great; if it was low, we wanted to stay away. We created labels for the range of each of the areas. The labels are listed below:

- **Cost Efficiency:** Inexpensive, Fair Tradeoff, Costly
- **Skill Set:** Thought Leadership, Development Opportunity, Maintenance
- **Partnership:** Transformative, Justifiable, Low Traction
- **Life Cycle:** Innovation, Transitional, Off-Ramp

Staying close to the outer edge was our goal. If most of the cost efficiency variables had a high score, we would call that set "inexpensive." If it was a mix of low values, we might call it a "fair tradeoff." We did not average the scores in one category to make that assessment. Instead, we used these labels more as talking points when we held portfolio review meetings.

So in short, we were looking for inexpensive, innovative technologies that would allow us to apply our thought leadership resulting in a transformative partnership for the group and the company. We stayed away from costly, declining technologies in maintenance mode that had low traction. Anything in between were points of discussion.

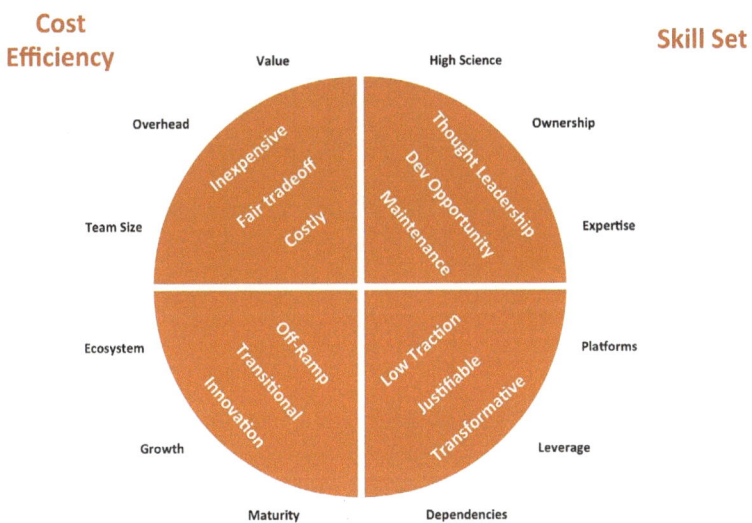

When you are creating a graph like the one above, you can place the words anywhere on the wheel. If you use a spreadsheet application, it will place the variables as predetermined by that application. As you will see later in the book, the placement of the twelve variables will be aligned by the clock: high science starts at twelve o'clock, ownership at one o'clock, and so on.

As mentioned before, you should select your own variables and labels. It should feel comfortable for the group. Once that is done, you are ready to start using the model.

A model has a set of variables that are assigned scores by the group. The scores are relative and intended to spur dialogue.

5

How Does the Model Work?

To recap, the model has four main areas. Each area has three variables that can have a score from zero, low, to ten, high. There are many ways of displaying the results of this information. I found using shapes (also called spider graphs) to be the most effective. Why? For many reasons. One, it is easy to understand that you are trying to achieve coverage in the areas you care about. Second, the shapes make it easy to remember. For some reason, very few people find meaning in a large set of numbers or a set of various-sized columns. Third, it is easy to compare shapes. You can quickly decide if a technology investment is viable or not, or if further data collection or discussions are needed. And finally, I think it looks great! Having spent decades presenting technical data to engineers, managers, and executives, this is my favorite! Keep in mind that using all these shapes when sharing information outside the group—meaning outside the group of people who understand the model and have come to appreciate it—may not always be the best approach. I suggest ideas for how that can be done later in the book.

Another question you may have is whether you should weight some of the categories more heavily than others. Perhaps the value category is more important than the number of dependencies? Yes, it may make more sense to weight them as you are thinking about getting more accurate numbers. However, keep in mind that this is not about the numbers. This is about making a simple model that people can understand and use as a "facilitator" when trying to make investment decisions. I did not find that weighting the numbers made our decisions any better.

An interesting observation about spider graphs is that you should not use the total area under the graph as a measure. Depending on where you place a variable, it may affect such calculations. You may, however, sum up all the values and compare the results with those of other technologies. You may also find it useful to focus on a few of the variables when assigning scores. For example, knowing the potential growth of a technology is different than knowing what new feature to add. So you may have to reach out to different groups with relevant expertise in order to complete the evaluations. If that is the case, be sure to explain the assigned scores to all contributors of this exercise.

I have found that it is useful to initially run through the exercise several times. Contributors often have an updated view after having had some time to reflect.

The Variables
Below are the categories and variables in a table form. It is useful to keep this within reach as you assign scores to the variables.

SHAPES Categories	
COST EFFICIENCY	
Team Size	Size of team needed to be successful
Overhead	Overhead in communication and coordination
Value	Perceived value, revenue or strategic
SKILL SET	
High Science	Cool stuff we like to do because it is challenging
Ownership	Level of ownership we have or can obtain
Expertise	Expertise in the group or can obtain
PARTNERSHIP	
Platforms	Number of supported platforms
Leverage	Number of supported product teams
Dependencies	Number of dependencies on other groups
LIFE CYCLE	
Maturity	Level of maturity for the technology today
Growth	Potential growth for this technology
Ecosystem	Level of definition/maturity of the ecosystem

Scoring

Taking the table above and adding the values for the ranges, we get this view:

SHAPES Scores	0	3.3	5	6.6	10
COST EFFICIENCY					
Team Size	≥ 15		8–10		2–3
Overhead	High		Medium		Low
Value	None		Medium		High
SKILL SET					
High Science	None		Medium		High
Ownership	None		Shared		Full
Expertise	Low		Medium		High
PARTNERSHIP					
Platforms	None	1		2	≥ 3
Leverage	None	5	10	15	≥ 20
Dependencies	≥ 3	2		1	None
LIFE CYCLE					
Maturity	≥ 10 years		Established		New
Growth	None		Medium		Significant
Ecosystem	Defined		Somewhat		Not Defined

This view is useful when scoring the technologies. Initially, it will seem confusing to assign a score of ten to a variable when the numbers are low. For example, you may assign a score of ten to team size when the team is small. At the same time, you are assigning a score of ten to platform when the number is high. The good news is that this quickly becomes a nonissue. All you have to do is to remind participants that the score of ten is a good thing for the group, while a lower score means more risk and more efforts and investments by the group.

In our case, we had variables that could only have certain values. For example, platform had values 0, 1, 2, or 3. The score on a ten-point scale then had to be 0, 3.3, 6.6, or 10. It may seem confusing, but it was not. It made perfect sense for us at the time. We did not want to make the model too streamlined. It was important to allow it to capture the ranges we were working with.

SHAPES	Tech A	Tech B	Tech C	Tech D	Tech E
COST EFFICIENCY					
Team Size	-	-	-	-	-
Overhead	-	-	-	-	-
Value	-	-	-	-	-
SKILL SET					
High Science	-	-	-	-	-
Ownership	-	-	-	-	-
Expertise	-	-	-	-	-
PARTNERSHIP					
Platforms	-	-	-	-	-
Leverage	-	-	-	-	-
Dependencies	-	-	-	-	-
LIFE CYCLE					
Maturity	-	-	-	-	-
Growth	-	-	-	-	-
Ecosystem	-	-	-	-	-

Next you score the technologies and place them into a spreadsheet program and generate the shapes. On the next few pages you will see some examples labeled 1 through 12 that I created based on my experiences of how these could look. Fill these out by talking about the relative numbers as compared to other technologies. You can either do it across—meaning by category—or you can score one technology before going on to the next. Often, you end up doing a mix of both approaches. Either way is fine as long as you keep it transparent. Sometimes, you may not be able to agree on a score. In that case, you can refer to an arbitrator as the final decision maker. This could be an expert in the area or a lead/manager. Occasionally, you may agree that you cannot assign the scores because you don't have enough information about a technology. In that case, you set those aside and return to them at a later point or you make your best guess and mark the evaluations as preliminary.

You should not make this a lengthy exercise. It is about rather quickly capturing what you as a group collectively already know. It is not about getting to accurate numbers. Based on my experience, you should be able to complete a twelve-technology review in two hours. Any longer, it becomes laborious and people will lose interest. A quick way of doing it is to share the view of the table and assign someone to enter the numbers. The person goes down the list and calls out the categories. Anyone can then suggest a score. If nobody else speaks up, then that becomes the score and you move on. If others have a different point of view, you allow some time for discussion. If after an agreed-upon time limit is reached, you make a decision or set it aside for a later review when more data is available. Make it a fun exercise. There are no right or wrong numbers. You are creating a picture of what you already know. After you have entered your numbers, it is best to take a break, even a day or two, before discussing the shapes and the various comparisons.

TECH	1	2	3	4	5	6	7	8	9	10	11	12
COST EFFICIENCY												
Team Size	6	7	6	5	6	7	5	5	5	6	7	5
Overhead	6	8	7	8	6	7	2	9	2	6	8	3
Value	8	9	9	8	6	7	8	8	3	8	5	3
SKILL SET												
High Science	8	8	8	10	9	7	7	6	7	5	5	7
Ownership	7	4	6	8	5	6	4	8	3	7	8	3
Expertise	9	8	6	9	7	6	5	9	8	9	9	3
PARTNERSHIP												
Platforms	10	10	6.6	3.3	10	6.6	10	3.3	10	6.6	6.6	6.6
Leverage	8	7	8	5	6	2	8	7	8	10	8	8
Dependencies	10	6.6	6.6	10	6.6	6.6	3.3	3.3	3.3	3.3	3.3	3.3
LIFE CYCLE												
Maturity	8	7	7	7	7	7	8	3	6	3	3	7
Growth	9	9	9	8	9	9	9	5	9	3	3	9
Ecosystem	8	9	8	6	8	9	9	5	8	3	3	9
SCORE												
Of total %	81	77	73	73	71	67	65	60	60	58	57	56

In the table above, my scores illustrate how this model works. I added the percentage of total points each technology could have. Twelve categories at ten points each is a maximum of 120. Instead of looking at total points, which will vary depending on how many categories you end up with, it is easier to think about the score in percentages Also, keep in mind that the total number of points does not have a real meaning other than being the sum of the individual scores.

Analysis
After you generate the graphs using a spreadsheet or similar application, you should lay them all out so it is easy to compare them. Now the fun starts. Analyze what each shape means, and suggest actions to take. It is best done with the same group that provided the input. Get them all together, and show the results. Spend some time understanding your

shapes. Probe into areas that do not make sense. Question areas that look too good.

On the next few pages, I've created the shapes for the twelve technologies. I have briefly discussed each one at a very high level. As you can see from the table scores, Tech 1 has the highest overall score at 81 percent, while Tech 12 has the lowest with 56 percent. This is just one data point. The more important item to focus on is the dialogue your team is having about the relative merits of each of them. You may be able to overcome some shortcomings in some areas, but not in others. Your investment decisions should be based on what you are able to do in the near term and the information you have available.

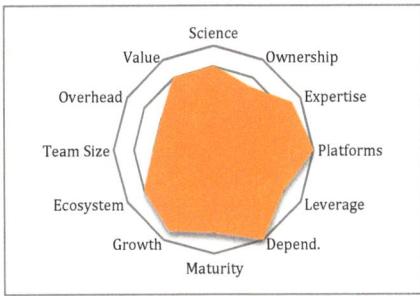

Tech 1 is a good candidate for investment. It does require a fair number of people and amount of overhead in interacting with other groups. Some level of shared ownership is required. The undefined ecosystem and potential growth are appealing.

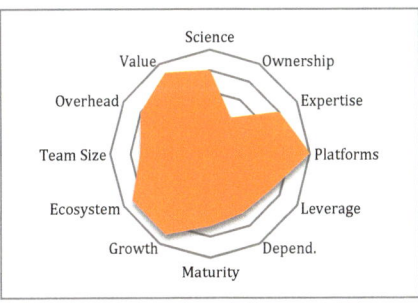

Tech 2 is similar to Tech 1, aside from the low level of ownership. Now it all depends on who the partner is. How has the past experience been in dealing with him or her as an owner?

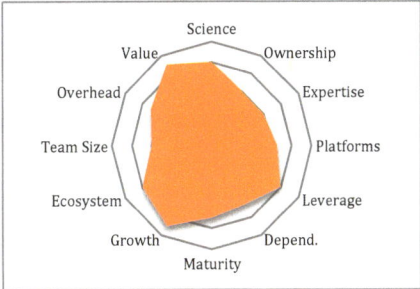

Tech 3 has an appealing growth, but the ownership is low, as is the level of expertise in the group. Will there be enough flexibility to grow expertise given that the control level may be low?

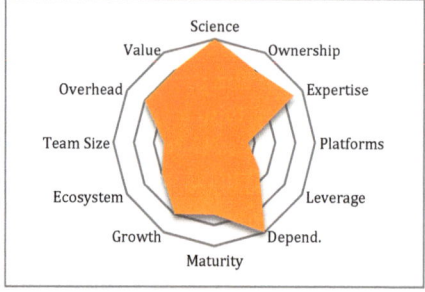

Tech 4 allows the group to dive deep into tough technical challenges. However, it is costly and supports only one platform. It is also in somewhat mature technology and ecosystem spaces.

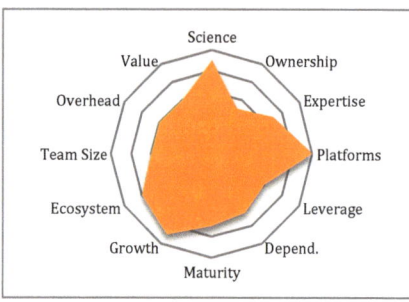

Tech 5 has several challenges ranging from lack of ownership, larger team needed, and many dependencies to low leverage. It does have technical depth and potenial growth, but overall, this area requires more consideration.

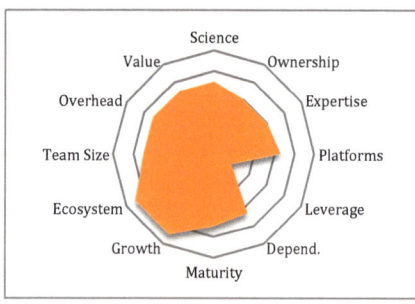

Tech 6 has a moderate profile, with low leverage. It has growth and ecosystem potential, but this may not be enough to compensate for the lack of leverage.

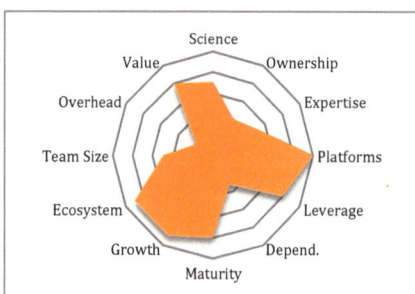

Tech 7 has several challenges. It requires a large team, new expertise, and much overhead. It also requires shared ownership. Avoid this one unless there is sufficient will to invest to bridge gaps and achieve potential growth.

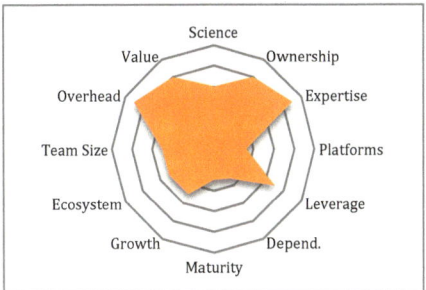

Tech 8 has an overall low profile. Only expertise and leverage are high. Unless something else surfaces, this is probably one to avoid.

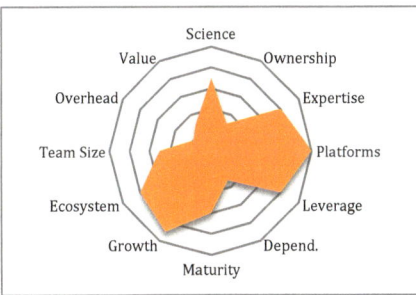

Tech 9 has the deep science that motivates the group but comes with a high price: lack of ownership, low value, and high cost.

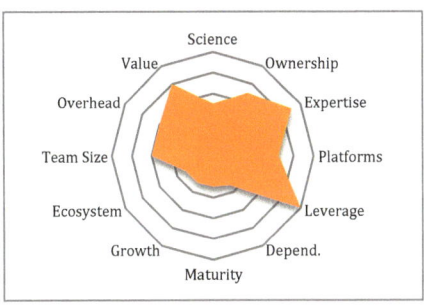

Tech 10 has high leverage, and the group has the expertise. However, the level maturity and the low growth makes it less interesting.

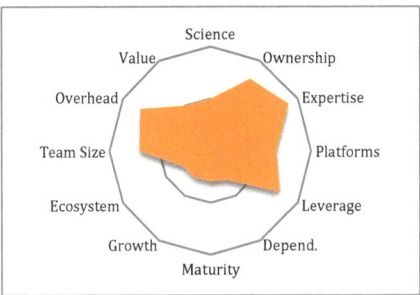

Tech 11 has a limited growth potential, low value, and low science. It has leverage and the group can get it done. The question is: Does it make sense for the company and the group to take this on?

Tech 12 has a growth future, deep science, and leverage. But the team lacks the expertise and it is costly. It also depends upon other groups. Investing will require deep pockets and dedication.

The fun part is analyzing and applying this knowledge. Where to start with the analysis? I would suggest starting at the top. Look at the overall numbers across all technologies. Look for patterns. Look at what you already are doing with the technologies you own. How are they stacking up to your ideals? Do they validate the model or contradict it? In the latter case, you may want to review your model. In the former, move on to see if these technologies are the right ones for you as compared with new ideas and opportunities waiting at the highway entrance.

In the next graph, I took all the shapes and put them together. That is the profile of my technology portfolio. For example, it looks like I am investing mostly in technologies that require medium-sized teams (nine o'clock). Is that good or bad? It is good in the sense that it is not too expensive, but bad in the sense that I am not investing in larger or smaller opportunities. Am I missing out on something because of that?

You can also see that everything done has the adequate skill level (twelve o'clock). That is great. However, does this mean that I am not investing in new areas, and that the group is not learning new skills and taking advantage of new technology trends? Is the group becoming stale? Should I start adding a set of technologies that requires a new skill set and is found in a growing space?

I have a few technologies, Tech 8 for example, that require a high level of overhead (ten o'clock). I have to work with a number of outside groups with many dependencies. This creates noise across my group. Is this something I should consider investing in? Sometimes, solving complicated problems requires a large amount of effort. Is the value there for the group and the company? Could this area be solved in a better way? Should we challenge the status quo and make a bold move to rid ourselves of the current implementation so we can move to a place with better overall scores?

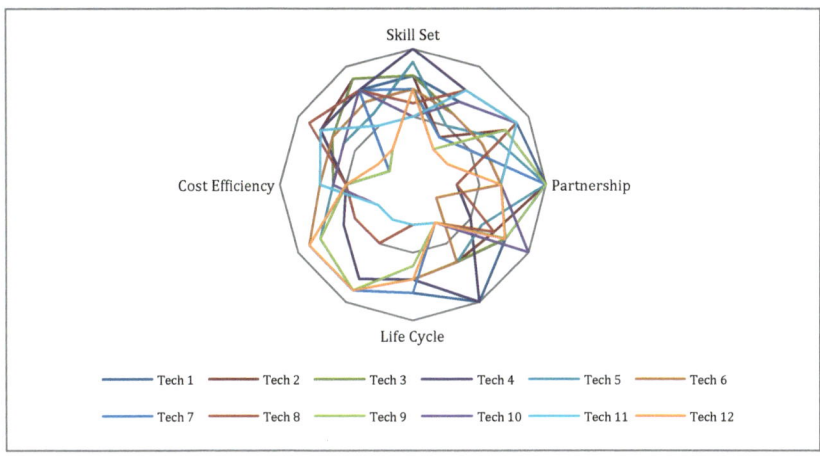

There are many ways of interpreting this information. It is just a starting point for the analysis. You should have these discussions with your group—the same group that provided the input to the portfolio. They will also know what is behind the numbers and can provide insight.

Another useful way of looking at this is to select a few technologies. In the next graph, I selected Tech 9 through 12.

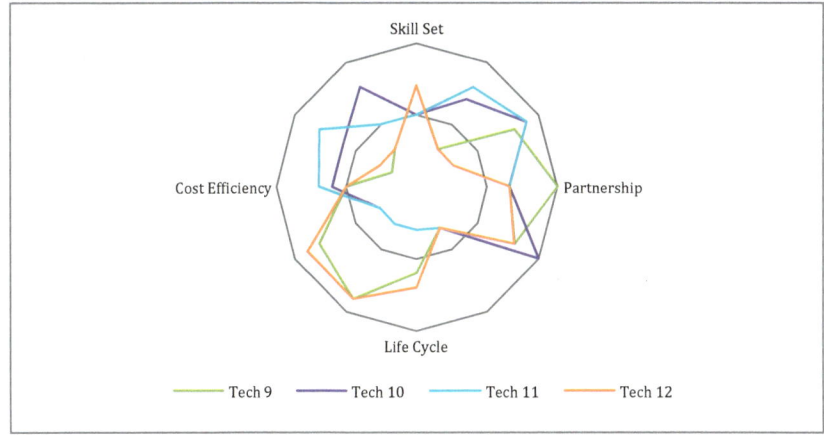

They all have high leverage (four o'clock). That is good. But at the same time, they all have many dependencies (five o'clock) and they are all in a relatively mature space (six o'clock).

Further Analysis

I spoke before about weighting certain variables more than others. That makes the model more complicated and difficult to understand. Another way of looking at variables you consider critical is to pull them out and examine them separately. In the following graph, I compare the team size (cost) to value. This is perhaps my key ROI slide. What are my minimum requirements? Should I should start from the the highest-ranked technology and look at all other variables in the model? These are just examples of how you can analyze the data.

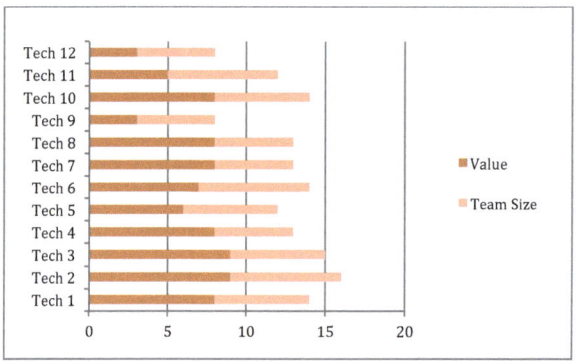

In the next graph I have listed high science and value. Those were the some of the original core variables we had to consider. You could drop technologies that did not meet your minimum criteria. I could say that a combined value of less than ten is too low. How do I arrive at ten? Only by experience. Over time, you see that certain profiles are more successful than others. The actual values are not the key. It is the relative values and their success rates that matter.

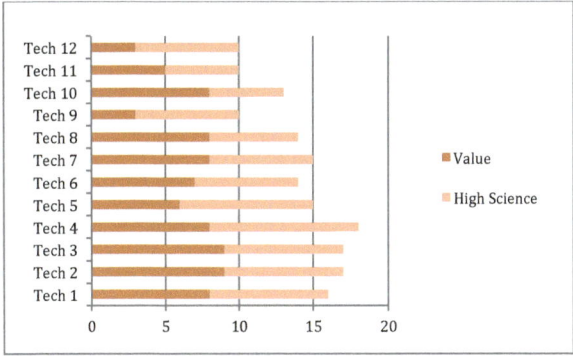

The same data is shown in the following graph. I have laid out the technologies in an X-Y diagram. Value is on the X-axis; science is on the Y-axis. You could add the actual numbers on the graph to make it clearer, but keep in mind that this is about relative values. I like this graph because it makes it very easy to compare technologies. And it is a great tool to use as part of analyzing the findings.

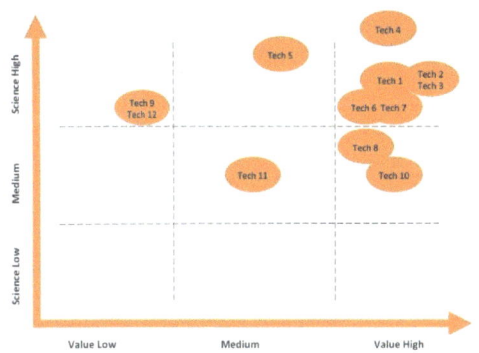

After you discuss your portfolio of technologies, it is time to make decisions. This does not mean that every person gets to vote. It means that every person gets to see how decisions are made and why. This is one of the most powerful outcomes from this exercise. It will allow you to get buy-in from the group on the new direction the group is moving. I would also suggest capturing decisions and making them available for the whole group, as well as sharing them with stakeholders, partners, and providers.

I would not use the above graphs as the initial way of communicating to outside groups. Unless they have been part of the process of capturing, analyzing, and deciding, it is difficult to understand why you made the decisions you made. In the next chapter, we will take a look at a few ways of sharing this information with other groups.

The model allows you to easily capture, display, compare, and analyze key success factors.

6

How Do You Implement the Model?

The implementation of a portfolio evaluation model can be accomplished in many ways. It works best when placed into a context for achieving a better outcome for the people in the group. If this is clearly communicated and you get the support from the group, you are off to a good start. The model is only as good as the information the group collectively can provide. Over the years, I have been able to use this model only because I had support and encouragement from the group.

To use a portfolio evaluation tool, you have to care for it every day. It must be fed and exercised. You collect data (feed) and evaluate the impact of the information (decision exercises). Then you bring it with you wherever you go. Soon, it becomes part of your daily life. In order to get to that point, here are some guiding principles on how to introduce a new tool to your group:

- Purpose: Optimize the impact on what the group is working on
- Transparency: Make the process and the data available to the group
- Fun: Make it easy to change the variables and the scores
- Consistency: Use the same group of people to update the scores
- Persistence: Use regularly as part of everyday work

Purpose is about knowing what is important and not. This must align with the accepted values of the group and what it is trying to become. It must support their goals. Very often, I see that the engineers or teams are very attached to their own project or technology. This is normal. They have spent time and energy getting it to where it is today. Making changes to their lives without an overall context is hard. It is important for the group to agree on the notion that a technology is a means to an end. If a technology no longer supports the end, then you should make changes. You should agree that not investing in one area also means that other areas will open up. You cannot create a situation in which a project ending equals the loss of jobs or movement of people to other groups. If that becomes the norm, you will never be able to collect real data or convince anyone that better opportunities are around. So, when you are looking at reducing investment in one area, you are also looking at increasing in another with the purpose of supporting the group's goals. Once this becomes accepted, teams are normally very open to moving from one technology into another with a brighter future. People want to help, and they want to be successful. Let them.

Transparency is making sure that everyone understands the purpose of this exercise and that data is made available. It should not be created by a secret society that surfaces once in a while with a message for the rest of the group. It must be clear that this information is useful for everyone. Everyone in the group must trust each other. It is about faith. If this is new to a group, give it a try. Over the years, I have never seen this being perceived as something sinister. I have only seen teams using it as a way of communication with each other. It is about the dialogue. Hence, it is important to allow as many people as possible to be part of this in some way. Not everyone has to be in the evaluation meetings, but everyone can provide feedback on the outcome. People can also use this on a smaller scale within their own teams or create a shape when they propose a new project.

Fun is the energy that drives this forward. Make it fun by creating real-time models that are updated once a variable changes its value. Make it visible online. Experiment with models to see what would happen if "this or that."

Consistency is important but not critical. As the use of the model grows, the consistency will decline. Just keep in mind that this is about the dialogue, not the numbers. You can always ask questions about any score at any time. You should always be able to dive into decisions to get more clarity. Sometimes, you will have different points of view. Sometimes, you will have to accept others getting their way. Sometimes, you will get your way. This is not about making everything fair; it is about making it possible.

Persistency is the glue. You will have to give it time. Not much will change after one or two meetings. It must become part of your overall methodologies. It will slowly make its way into the dialogues of the group and become a language that more and more people will know and understand. If you keep at it, you will reach the tipping point. There is no way back once you have started looking at technology more holistically. There will not be a future where you can imagine evaluating a possibility solely based upon the technical skills of the group or the size of the opportunity. You know that success requires many things to go right, whereas failure requires just one thing to go wrong.

Getting Started

Implementation may require a one-day offsite. First, you must allow participants to express their general view about portfolio management and share their concerns about using a new approach. These concerns should be captured and addressed. Here are some that I have heard over the years:

- What is the point?
- Another exercise?
- How long will this last?
- Nothing will change anyway.
- I don't feel comfortable using numbers as a basis for making decisions.
- Numbers will be used to make decisions that turn against us.
- Numbers will be too complicated for us to understand.
- Only people in charge or who are aggressive get heard.
- We don't know enough to be able to conduct evaluations.

If you follow the guiding principles presented earlier in this chapter, most of the above concerns will be addressed. There are two categories of concern I would like to discuss because you may not recover from them if you ignore them. The first is that some people may use this to validate their own point of view, pushing their own agenda forward. They could use part of what is in this model and ignore the rest. They may support the people who are working on their projects and starve others. If you see this happening, you have to make the behavior stop or remove those people from the effort. You must convince all parties that the purpose of this tool is to strip away bias toward areas that someone is deeply invested in. The goal is to get collective clarity of the world so that, as a group, you can be best positioned for future success, regardless of past investments. The world is changing fast. I have seen over and over again organizations and technologies being removed or abandoned because people held on to the past for too long. Why do this to yourself? Mostly, because it is easy and comfortable. The longer you procrastinate, though, the more time you will spend ignoring the future. So it becomes a choice: changes that you drive or changes cast upon you by someone else.

The second category is that the data can be used against the contributors. I see this every day. When you report on a feature that is late, your leaders will ask you to work over the weekend, or they will put pressure on you to come up with a workaround. Do you need this kind of leadership support? I will say that most teams and individuals know how to address this situation. In some cases, they will need some support, but most often, it is just a matter of giving them some time and encouragement. So what is happening here? I will put forth that we are the source of this issue. We feed the leadership data about what we are doing, such as schedules, bugs, features, resources, issues, and risks. This is what everybody does. The question is why? Will this information be useful for the company leadership? Yes, to some degree, but is this what they should be doing— stepping in to solve your problems?

I will suggest that you look at your leadership through a different lens. Ask, what is their role? They should focus on steering the company in the direction of success. They should focus on the vision and the goals, the business models, and the portfolio of technologies they are investing in. They should not help you ship projects. So, change the dialogue. Move it into an area that is helpful for all involved. Insist on being part of the portfolio discussion. Set up agreements on how this should be done. It could be done as part of the planning process. Some companies do this often, others once a year. Agree on goals and road maps, but stay away from detailed deliverables. But do not surprise them with a snapshot of your evaluations in the middle of a major product launch. Timing is critical.

There is always some level of resistance. This is normal. It is part of critical thinking. Everyone asks, "What will this do for me? Is it worth my time?" Also expect that many will see this as an opportunity to finally become part of a dialogue about their destiny. They will support your idea and charge ahead. Great! Let them lead the way. However, it is important that everyone moves at the same pace and is part of the dialogues. This is not a race and definitely not a sprint; it is a journey that will require some level of planning.

Some Process
As you get ready to roll out the model you should consider defining a few simple rules. Don't create too many rules and keep them easy to implement and maintain. Once you have them in place, you can start diving into areas to investigate further or make and communicate your investment decisions.

Here are a few rules I will suggest you start with:

- A list of contributors to the portfolio evaluation model
- A set of steps/rules for how and when to contribute to the model
- A person who keeps the master copy updated in a central place
- Agreement on how to share/distribute the content of the model

The Highway

A simple way of communicating portfolio decisions is to use the highway concept. You are on the highway, coming on, or exiting. The same goes for a technology. It is active, it is new with growing investment, or it is mature with lowered investment. You can, of course, also be off the highway with no resources or support. You may then use additional categories such as new or end of life (EOL). That sends a clear message about a technology's future potential. If EOL, the technology is not going anywhere. If new, it is just an idea that may or may not enter the highway. As mentioned in chapter 2, these are the labels we have found worked well in the highway concept:

- On-Ramp
- Highway: Invest, Steady-State, Maintain
- Off-Ramp

On-ramp means newer ideas that are in development, not a version 1.0 yet. You may have to indicate a time line for release. On-ramp is a way of showing new ideas and preparing internal customers for upcoming features. You can use this to show any idea you have, but that can quickly become too much. We had our new idea process that captured ideas and moved them to the on-ramp when ready.

On highway, invest was a category of technologies that were newer, growing in use or investment. They took priority over competing work in other areas. For steady-state, we allowed any type of work to be done as defined by the current team size. They would use an Agile process and place requests in the backlog. In maintain, we limited efforts to critical fixes. There were no new features added (ideally). It was about keeping it as is. The team sizes were small, or these technologies were supported by teams that had other responsibilities.

Off-ramp is about showing technologies that are moving to no support sometime in the future. You should add a time line and what will happen to that technology. For example, it could be placed in an open source environment, parked on a server for use by anybody (no support), or simply removed from the server with no access.

So when you are communicating investment decisions, it is easy to show where technologies are placed. They may move over time, but that is easily captured (and tracked for backward-looking analysis). Once you have this view, you can use it for further analysis. You could, for example, show the total investment in each category in total headcount or money. You could show the percentage distribution of total investment in each category. That is useful as it shows how you are managing your portfolio. Often, a company would like to see a certain profile, such as 10 percent of all investment on new ideas. Or it may want to move into a new area and reduce the investment in the maintain category. The table below captures what my portfolio could look like in the highway concept. There is no formula for placing technologies. The placements are the outcome of group discussions and decisions.

On-Ramp	HIGHWAY			Off-Ramp
	Invest	Steady	Maintain	
Tech 1	Tech 3	Tech 5	Tech 8	Tech 10
Tech 2	Tech 4	Tech 6	Tech 9	Tech 11
		Tech 7		Tech 12

The Off-Ramp

If you are working in an established company, you probably already have a number of commitments tied to your portfolio of technologies. It is rather easy to make a decision on investing in something new because very often this brings excitement and hope for the future. It can be difficult to move a technology onto the off-ramp. I have seen this done in many ways. At one end, you get a one-line email that says the technology/product is no longer supported and good luck! If you are a current user or have some dependencies, you are now forced to spend time resolving your dependencies. It may mean very little, or you may get this message just as you are ready to ship and this technology is embedded into your product. On the other hand, I have seen this done over a longer period with input from stakeholders and an ongoing discussion about the overall portfolio, not about one technology. With that level of agreement it is clear for all what the direction is and why. And when the time comes to move the technology off the highway, everybody is prepared.

Then I have seen everything in between. The important question to ask when stopping support for a technology is whether you are losing trust from your customers or stakeholders as a results of your actions. If you only make decisions from your point of view—meaning, quickly moving technologies off the highway—then your next new idea shared with your customers will be tough to present. They will remember and assume that this may happen again. It can be a tough hurdle to overcome.

The On-Ramp

On the other hand, it is critical to have a path for new ideas to enter the highway. Setting up a review and providing feedback to teams is simply not enough. You must have the ability to implement decisions, or you will waste people's time and they will stop coming to you for support. They will instead ask other groups or move underground.

At one time, we had fifty new ideas presented by fifty smaller virtual teams. They were all looking to get funded and place their ideas into products. They faced three major issues. One was that most teams did not know how to validate the idea. It seems simple. Get customer feedback and adjust. It is not. It requires skills and dedication. Then, for those who passed that hurdle, they got stuck in creating a prototype or something that could showcase the new idea. Unless you have something convincing, it is very difficult to get funding. Lastly, it was very difficult to develop a new product that was outside established products' business model. This was not only limited to our group, but applied to the whole company. Why was this the case? There was no funding or model to get this done at scale. There was support and encouragement but low chance that someone could bring a totally new product or technology idea onto the highway. So how did new ideas come into being? For the most part, they were brought in by someone who managed a team that already owned a technology or product. They had the ability to add new features or explore new solutions within their area.

To encourage innovation, we set up a group that could support new ideas by removing hurdles. That in itself requires investment. Once that is underway, you still need the ability to accept new ideas onto the highway. The easiest way of getting that done is to move low-scoring technologies to the right in the model, toward the off-ramp, and at the same time allow new technologies onto the on-ramp. In this way you are keeping overall portfolio investment stable, hence, avoiding a delay by asking for more people.

The new idea stage is another model in itself. It is not your portfolio, but a place where new ideas come from. At some point they can move from this early stage onto the on-ramp. How you organize that could vary from almost no oversight to a very rigid process. It all depends on your how your company thinks about innovation. Some companies allow employees to work on anything. The idea is that nobody knows what the next big thing is, so why try to control it? Other groups have clear gates the teams must go through to progress toward an on-ramp.

What we ended up with was a combination. Over the years, we saw a very low hit rate for new ideas that were too far from the key company goals. They were great ideas, but they required significant investments in a new direction. If you are faced with too many of these types at the same time, you can easily get stuck in chaos. We saw a very high hit rate when the ideas were very close to an existing technology, product, or business model. These ideas were much easier to implement, as they could leverage current infrastructure. So we had choices to make: go for something big that had a very low chance of success, or perhaps focusing on gaining several smaller wins? Or something in between? Sometimes, this choice was not clear at the time someone presented an idea. Hence, a framework was needed.

What we ended up using was Shapes, a portfolio evaluation approach that also works on new ideas. In addition to Shapes, we also provided guidance to the group. We defined technology tracks that were aligned with company strategy and goals. It is always much easier to obtain funding, resources, and support when you are working under an umbrella that the whole company supports. We normally would have three to five tracks in a given year. They would have easy-to-remember names with descriptions covering type of usage, technology underpinnings, and deployment methods. This guidance was very much appreciated by the group. The one challenge with this approach was that you could end up with parts of your technology portfolio outside these tracks, meaning that the message you sent could be interpreted as: "You are not a valued member. You are not supporting company goals." Therefore, pick the tracks carefully.

The other issue that tracks bring up is the part of the portfolio called maintenance and off-ramp. Nobody wants to work on old stuff, things that are not valued by the company. To combat this, you have to spend time assuring the group that this is how a company becomes successful. Many mature technologies make money that is critical for new ideas to take hold. At the same time, we all should expect to be responsible for moving a technology through its phases until it is no longer in use. We found that giving everyone opportunities to work on newer technologies or just new ideas, even in a very limited capacity, went a long way.

A very useful way of thinking about investing in new technologies is to refer to Jim Collins's book *Great by Choice*. He says to first fire bullets then cannonballs. Before investing massive amounts of time and money into a new project, test the waters. Once you have calibrated your aim, give it your best.

Sharing the Portfolio
What else could be shared about your portfolio? I have found it useful to select two variables many consider relevant or important. Often, they are about cost and return. They could also be about new directions or technologies that the company wants to invest in. If you have an audience that cares about these variables, then you could use the X-Y diagrams as shown earlier in the book.

Regardless of the format, the most important questions to ask are what message do you want to send and why? Always seek to address key issues or opportunities. Do not share all that you are capable of collecting. Do not use this as an opportunity to show off your skills. Keep the purpose crystal clear. Otherwise, you are crowding the communication channels. Giving too much information too often without purpose should be avoided. Do not become the person who overwhelms. Instead, become someone who has an important message to convey that solves a problem or reveals a new opportunity.

Before sharing your portfolio evaluations, consider the following questions:

- Who is your audience?
- What do they know about you and your group?
- What is important for them?
- What decisions are they seeking to make?
- How do they prefer to receive information?

These are just some of the questions to ask, but they are critical. You don't want to find out later that all the work you have put into preparing your information was wasted, or worse, used to make critical decisions it was not meant for.

The assumed goal behind your efforts is to optimize your portfolio. The audience of your information should have the same goal; that is why you are sharing. But they may have questions, constraints, or new opportunities to present. In any case, be prepared to own your data. If at any point you cannot explain what you have created, you are jeopardizing the group. Therefore, it matters who the messenger is. It must be someone who can explain how the data was created, what it means, and why decisions were made.

In keeping with communicating effectively, make your presentations as short as possible. Keep your key points constrained to three to five pages, but list where additional information can be found. Most people appreciate a to-the-point presentation and discussion. In my experience, when sharing this type of information with another group, you seldom leave page 2. The audience will have questions; they want to discuss what is on their minds. Be prepared to engage them. Do not focus on the presentation itself, as it is only a means to an end. Focus on your goals.

Implement the model by engaging the group and sharing results widely. Stay focused on decisions, and do not flood communication channels with data.

7

Going Beyond the Evaluation Model

There you have it, a fairly simple approach to creating a portfolio evaluation model. Make it fit your world. Make it work for you. Make it part of what you do every day.

Now the bigger question: how do you make it successful in your group and your company in the long run? Every day, we have more things to do than we have time. We have many ideas that could help us become more effective. We have many opportunities that could expand our options. We have choices to make. The important question is how can this evaluation model coupled with a portfolio discipline drive your company forward in making better products that your customers will love?

Look at your surroundings as a series of systems. Your family is a system. Our schools are systems. Your work—your company—is a system. An organization is a system with a purpose, people, processes, and outcomes. Combined, it behaves in a somewhat prescriptive way. Its boundaries limit its behavior for good or for bad. It is just like a boat— there are only so many things it can do once it leaves the harbor.

Think about an investment as a change to a system, not as an isolated decision. A decision to move people from one area to another will have an equal and opposite reaction. Therefore, manage your system. Do not manage everything as individual items with no dependencies. Everything is part of the whole. Without the whole, the parts cannot exist.

Changing a portfolio from one profile to another requires a number of steps in all corners of an organization. Therefore, you must manage these

43

changes for the longer term and not focus on only one project for a shorter time.

The Competitive Advantage of Nations, by Michael Porter, does a great job of arguing why companies from certain countries are doing well in the global marketplace. He looks at his system of four interlinked factors:

- Firm strategy, structure, and rivalry: direct competition makes firms improve productivity and innovation.
- Demand conditions: the more demanding the customers, the greater the pressure to improve their competitiveness via innovative products.
- Related supporting industries: access to upstream or downstream industries allows for the exchange of ideas.
- Factor conditions: these include skilled labor, capital, and infrastructure.

His model is not without fault or criticism. But it does offer an example of how companies can assess their own situation as compared to companies from other nations. By using his model, you could learn if a company has some advantages, and therefore, an increased chance of global success. More relevant to this book is that the model put forth by Michael Porter opens the door for looking inside your own company. There are certain conditions that give you an edge. Others may not. For example, he argues that innovation benefits from dialogues with partners and suppliers (upstream and downstream industries). The more, the better. Does this not also apply inside a company? I believe that innovation is a result of dialogues across different groups and disciplines. The more dialogue, the better. The same can be said for skills, money, and tools. The more you have, the better. If you have demanding customers, they expect you to deliver better products.

So in short, Michael Porter says that success and competitive advantages are linked. In his case, he was comparing companies. In this book, it is about comparing your company today and your company in the future. In order to create a picture of your desired future state you should focus on competitive advantages, not only on specific technologies or products. The assumption here is that if you have all the right conditions, the right products will emerge. Why? Because you are managing your technology portfolio as a system. Once you have identified your desired future conditions, you validate and document them. Include them in your picture of the future state of your company. That becomes your vision.

Where do you start? First, consider your system at work. Very often, short-term problems and high-level goals are what drive the majority of the activities in a company. The project that is seen as the most important at the time gets all the attention. Everyone looks at the number of open issues and the next release date. If there is a bottleneck, other groups are asked to help out. If someone is not on top of the latest updates from "the project," he or she is seen as an outsider. At the same time, the higher level goals are often stated as *grow revenue*, *beat the competition*, or *innovate*. Unless someone has turned them into goals that your group can reach, you are now trapped in a perpetual high-stress situation of helping out the most critical project in absence of a clear direction.

In order to avoid this scenario, everyone in the company should have a well-defined part to play. And everyone needs to know how all the parts fit into the whole system. A portfolio evaluation model supported by a portfolio management discipline is the engine that drives this system. The large system consists of four groups held together by an operational model. Those groups are what makes a company. They are:

- Customers: companies and individuals who use the products and services from your company.
- Partners: companies and individuals who are supporting you in some way to run your company.
- Employees: the people who are paid to deliver products and services and do everything in between required to run a company.
- Stakeholders: the owners or people with special interests in the success of the company.

The operational model that holds them together consists of a number of key parts. They are:

- Purpose: This is what defines the company. In this category, you often find vision and mission statements. Every company must know why it exists and what it is trying to become. If this is not understood and embodied by the leadership team, the four groups will soon drift apart and conflict will arise.
- Roles and responsibilities: This is very seldom documented anywhere in a company. Often, the organizational chart is the rendition of who is responsible for what. An organizational structure should be put in place to support key roles and their duties. Therefore, it should be created after you have decided on what is needed to make your company successful.
- Methodologies and tools: Everything in the company should be focused on helping people in their roles. Every process should be linked directly to a role, and every tool should make the task simpler and more effective.
- Organizational structure: Once you have defined the preceding three areas, you create your organization. The benefit of keeping it separate from the above is so that when changes are needed, when things are not going well in

one area, or when you have a new opportunity in another, you can more easily locate where action might be required. Perhaps it is just a process change. Perhaps a tool did not work out well. As a last resort, change the organization. Why last resort? Because it is expensive to regroup people without knowing if the benefits will outweigh the cost.

In this system you have two big decisions to make and many smaller ones. The big decisions are where is the company today, and where do you want the company to be in the future. You need to paint a picture of these two states of the company. Use any language you want. In the end, it must be clear to everyone what the difference is between today and the desired future state. And don't forget to prominently include competitive advantages. Once this is completed, you have to decide on how to arrive at the future state. Make a list of initiatives that are designed to change your system. For each initiative, capture goals, actions, drivers, and a time line. Review progress, make changes, and share successes. Hold drivers accountable.

As with the technology evaluation model, the important part of the company operational model is the discussion around it. It is meant to engage all groups around common goals. It should allow all parties to focus on the end state: a system that can produce products and services your customer will love, a system that is designed to work better than the competition's. Getting there will take some time. It will require a deep level of determination and focus. This transformation must become an integral part of how the company is run. Is it easy? No, but it is very possible to achieve!

A technology evaluation model can become the cornerstone of a company's operational model.

ABOUT THE AUTHOR

Erik Boe is currently working at VMware defining and implementing portfolio management and software delivery models. Prior to that he was at Adobe, where he was part of a global technology group delivering technologies to all Adobe product teams. This central and unique position enabled him to gain deep insight into technology portfolio management and innovation across the company. Before joining Adobe he was with a startup struggling to deliver Internet storage solutions. He started his career with Apple. He was there before, during, and after the company's turnaround, first in the MacOS group and later in the hardware division. He had roles ranging from software engineer to manager and program manager, driving company-wide efforts focused on optimizing technology delivery and innovation. He has a master's in international business from Pepperdine University and a bachelor of computer science from the University of California, Santa Barbara. He grew up in Norway and later moved to California to join the personal computer revolution. He currently lives in the Bay Area, California, with his wife, three children, a dog, and a cat.